3

D0832217

Samarkand

KATE CLANCHY was born in Glasgow in 1965 and was educated in Edinburgh and Oxford. She won an Eric Gregory Award in 1994. Her first book, *Slattern*, was published in 1996 and won the Forward Prize for Best First Collection, the Saltire Prize for the Scottish First Book of the Year, a Scottish Autumn Book Award and a New London Writers Award. In 1997 she was awarded a Somerset Maugham Award and was shortlisted for the John Llewellyn Rhys Prize. After several years in the East End of London, she moved to Oxford in 1998 and works there as a teacher and freelance writer.

KATE CLANCHY

Samarkand

PICADOR

First published 1999 by Picador
an imprint of Macmillan Publishers Ltd
25 Eccleston Place, London SW1W 9NF
Basingstoke and Oxford
Associated companies throughout the world
www.macmillan.co.uk

ISBN 0 330 37194 0

1 3 5 7 9 8 6 4 2

A CIP catalogue record for this book is available from
the British Library.

Printed and bound in Great Britain by
Mackays of Chatham plc, Chatham, Kent

For Matthew Reynolds

Acknowledgements

I should like to thank the newspapers and magazines in which some of these poems first appeared, including the *Scotsman*, the *New Statesman*, the *Independent*, the *Independent on Sunday*, *Poetry Review*, *Verse*, *Thumbscrew* and *Critical Quarterly*.

'Hometime' and 'Act 2' were first published in *New Scottish Writing*, ed. Harry Ritchie.

'The Acolyte' was first broadcast on BBC Radio 4. 'The Bridge Over the Border' was first broadcast on BBC World Service.

I am grateful to the London Arts Board for the New Writers Award which made finishing this manuscript much easier. The generosity of the British Council and the Society of Authors' Somerset Maugham Award have together allowed me to at least *fly* over Samarkand.

I would like to thank Don Paterson, Colette Bryce and Matthew Reynolds for their criticism and advice.

Contents

The NewHome Cabaret

The Bridge Over the Border

Here, I should surely think of home –
my country and the neat steep town
where I grew up: its banks of cloud,
the winds and changing, stagey light,
its bouts of surly, freezing rain, or failing that,

the time the train stuck here half an hour.
It was hot, for once. The engine seemed
to grunt and breathe with us,
and in the hush, the busker at the back
plucked out *Scotland the Brave*. There was

a filmic, golden light and the man opposite
was struck, he said, with love.
He saw a country in my eyes.
But he was from Los Angeles,
and I was thinking of another bridge.

It was October. I was running to meet a man
with whom things were not quite settled,
were not, in fact, to ever settle, and I stopped
halfway to gaze at birds – swallows
in their distant thousands, drawn

to Africa, or heat, or home, not knowing
which, but certain how. Shifting on the paper sky,
they were crosses on stock-market graphs,
they were sand in a hoop shaken sideways,
and I stared, as if panning for gold.

To Travel

(after Gösta Ågren)

If you should go to Samarkand
you might find Scheherazade
reproduced a thousand times,
tinsel-clad, in gift shops,
and Al-al-Din's gold-plated domes
slung with Soviet tourist signs
and tarnished, on a brassy sky.

But staying is a kind of leaving.
From here, the fields of Oxfordshire
stretch already sovereign-golden.
And when the hay is rolled in bales
like wheels, and your eye runs on
black tractor rills to autumn's bare horizon,
there shall burn there Samarkand,

and Samarkand, and Samarkand.

Burglar Alarm, E1

It seems to be something
they're used to ignoring
in the stalls, curry houses,
Pound-Busters for Housewives,
the glassy, funereal Arcades
of the Whitechapel Waste,
East Aldgate, Brick Lane –
this pulsing alarm, saying
*opened and taken, broken
and stolen,* again and again.

And that, furthermore,
they give no time to pondering –
the grandsons of pogroms,
calling out prices, the Somali
women with shopping
and veils, the Bengali men
clasping hands in a bargain,
all stilled in the milk
of a mild autumn evening –
this modern conundrum:

whether the swallows
dispersing like gunshot
on the smoke-stack clouds,
the bloody sky,
have recently learned
to sound like a siren, or
whether the siren
is intended to mimic
the hierarchic, repeating,
screams of migration.

History Lesson

Even the wretched want amusement!
So, each Whit, ten thousand walked
from Aldgate Pump to Wanstead Flats.
Their best-shoe, patched-boot, barefoot
tracks rubbed each other down to dust
along the ancient cattle route.

There – as if ten thousand souls
were not enough – were waxworks
and a tent selling half-hours with the dead.
Hordes not-lost-but-gone-before
were recognized by their relatives,
though each ghost wore the same white dress.

Next door, the Instant Portrait Stall
lent the punters a hat, flashed the usual stuff
with the bird and the hood, then thrust
the same blurred print of a girl in her best,
taken up West, years ago, in hand
after hand, and got away with it,

as if the poor all shared one smile,
one face. Also, there was Aunt Sally,
the Hall of Mirrors, the Coconut Shy,
and Shooting Gallery, and
the Miracle Man with Microscope
who would, for a penny, demonstrate

that each hand was a land, each crease
which ran from thumb to wrist, wide
as the Thames or the Whitechapel Waste,
and teemed with things which seemed
to live, were footprint-shaped,
and were dirt, in fact.

War Poetry

The class has dropped its books. The janitor's
disturbed some wasps, broomed the nest
straight off the roof. It lies outside, exotic
as a fallen planet, a burst city of the poor;
its newsprint halls, its ashen, tiny rooms
all open to the air. The insects' buzz
is low-key as a smart machine. They group,
regroup, in stacks and coils, advance
and cross like pulsing points on radar screens.

And though the boys have shaven heads
and football strips, and would, they swear,
enlist at once, given half a chance,
march down Owen's darkening lanes
to join the lads and stuff the Boche –
they don't rush out to pike the nest,
or lap the yard with grapeshot faces.
They watch the wasps through glass,
silently, abashed, the way we all watch war.

When my Grandmother
said she should never have left

New Zealand, land of her birth,
breakfast lamb-chops,
and frequent, casual earthquakes –
it frightened us.
To cast her net so very wide
over years, decades, lives –
was like a ground tremor starting,
spreading quick as misgivings,
wrinkling oceans, rumpling borders,
spiralling out of the southern hemisphere
to compass Moscow and the War,
lap at England, Hampshire, here.

And then to let the sonar rings
reach our feet and pass us,
loop us, to pull them back
with that single gesture,
uptailing me, my cousins, brother,
into new volcanic fissures,
dowsing my father, uncle, aunt
in the China Sea till they paled to thoughts;
letting all our books and paintings
bob to other hands, like jetsam,
to push even my grandfather under
with his Captain's hat, his careful letters;

to furl all this in her fist at the epicentre,
where she stood, fifteen,
a skinny, straight-browed girl,
waiting for plates to settle flat
on the dresser, her cup
to click in the dent in the saucer,
the framed map of the Empire
to sway back horizontal,
for everything to be
as if nothing had happened,
and then to toss the twisted paper
in the grate to light a fire, later –

that shook me.

My Grandfather

His head was grand and mottled as a planet.
There were no maps: his rage sprang up
mysterious as geysers. The continents
were dark where his several brothers
lived (though Uncle James from Africa
once showed up in the flesh) and if
there were, in the frozen poles, the hole
he'd put his father in, long ago, I never knew
nor dared to ask. He was munificent
and vast. This is all I know for sure:

Grandad looked like old Duke Wayne
and shot birds with the Earl of Cairn.
He had cigars and a Jaguar, and his father
was a gas fitter. He beat us all at dominoes,
but drew black/black one day and died.
Because of him we're not self-made.
He left us that, Aunt Katie's rug
and a drawer full of cashmere socks,
luxurious and muffling, easily worn to holes.

Hometime

When my grandfather died he saw,
he said, not Death's bare head, but aunts,
his antique aunts in crackling black,
come to call him back from play.

Act 2

If you aged the way they do on stage –
came home to find the set had changed,
new chairs, bright walls you didn't choose,
and the heads turned towards you doused
in powder, as if the ceiling had fallen
in a blizzard of plaster and they'd sat on,

too stupid, too surprised, to unarch their brows
or flex their faces, claw off the latex jowls,
the padded chins and pencilled wrinkles,
wipe the dust from their rheumy eyes –

would you laugh, do you think, or walk
back through the paper door and run amok
behind the scenes, locate the lout
in charge of lights, the wiseass who wrote
the script, demand the truth, the truth, or
ram a fist through those crisp unlikely walls? Or

would you know the scene for one you'd practised,
pick up your cue and cross to Mother
and know, too, as you stooped to kiss her,
the flat hoarse voice whispering your lines?

Deep Blue

(*in memoriam* John Blau, 1964–1991,
and for his widow, Jackie Molloy)

I was not surprised to hear how the rest survived,
were anthropologists in Vegas, parents
or beat poets, had turned heterosexual
and got tenure at Yale; how even the tortoise
we fished out of the turtle-tank
in that upstate, backstreet pet shop,
still trundles round, armoured and mechanical,
drearily alive, while you, you had died.

You were always the one everyone chose.
The athlete, the actor, the centre of the photo
with your arms on many shoulders. I can hear
your rapid, Disney laugh, see you
reading Shakespeare in a college letter jacket.
It was Indian summer, you strutted
on a wall, your intent, coiled back,
dark, mobile face, inhabiting the Fool.

It was the mechanism got me – the intricate
encroachment of the thing. A single night
in Texas! Nobody could die from that
unless somebody planned it, unless
Death crouched a long time at his chessboard,
working it out. Unless he called to you
in passing, patted the café seat beside him,
quaint, European, an old man in the sun.

Then offered easy odds and gambits
of top roles and turtles, hooked your knight,
sipped coffee, let his bishop slide,
chuckled and checked you, shut
his rheumy, hooded eyes. You were easily bored.
You must have laughed that laugh and
leant across, twitched the king, slapped
the clock and turned to the street, to the girls

and the flowers, stretched your basketball limbs
tucked your thumbs in your pockets,
young, young, all Bogart, American.
You would have smiled when he murmured
your name. And I am shocked when I imagine
the click of wood on wood, and your face
when you recognized the absolute design
of his swift and final black rook move.

The Invisible Man

It was the bandages that book got right.
We're none of us quite here, alone –
the way we pat our cheeks at night
to check our flesh still clothes the bone.

Record Low

There was a father, mid-west France –
moustached, thickset, with garlic breath,
the very *bon papa*, or *paysan* we learned
about in school – who, after weeks
of freakish cold, walked out at eight
to rare fresh snow, and laughed
and called in sick and fetched his daughter,
two, to see him build a snowman.

She was tiny, anoraked, entranced,
clapping mittens inches long, licking
her first snowball. She watched Papa's boots,
his straining, rounded bum, march a path
across the garden, saw, between his legs,
the snow roll grow, creaking like a yacht deck.
It swelled to spaceship, planet-size.
They were going for the record.

She ran to help, wee arms outstretched,
to measure its vast belly. But Papa was lost,
obsessed, and didn't stop till he'd plugged
in the twiggy hands, the coal, short-sighted eyes,
the rotten-toothed agape grin. He turned
and she was nowhere. He searched,
of course, and called up friends, told
his already-sobbing, knowing wife.

She thrust her apron in her mouth,
watched men spread across
black-bordered fields, grow distant,
tiny, Breughelesque. She saw,
perhaps a dozen times, a slender ghost
dart from a dyke or a snow-blocked ditch,
walk, silently as Wenceslas,
a pace or two behind them.

At dusk, the landscape dimmed
like stacked-up silky scarves.
The snowman stood athwart the gate,
a crossed-through eight, a local god
grown goitrous on the gibbet.
Fresh ice had spiked his coat:
when she beat him with her bare fists,
it grated them like onions.

The baby, when they prised her out,
had open arms, an open mouth, frosted over
in soft focus, like the closing stills
of films, the near embrace of memory.
She'd been her Papa's doll, his angel,
and his butterfly. Late that night,
the water main cracked beneath the square.
The streets flooded and the taps ran dry.

Nine Months

He grew thin as she grew great,
ran, got back in shape –
like when we met, she said
at first, but glimpsed,
stretching in the street light,
the silhouette of a boy
some years before that.

He ran each night – despite
the growing winter dark,
the rounded weight of black
which pressed on the sparse-lit,
urban park, would sprint
the curving miles of path
as if stretching for the finish tape.

And if he thought his chest
might hone to bone, and
file down to a blade, or a sliver,
and whether he meant the knife
to cut the cord, or just to slice the air,
then hover, flicker, disappear –
was something not discussed.

The Natural History Museum

They are glassed and boxed like childhood,
the dead creatures in their pastoral
dance: the grinning fox and pouting squirrel,
the ferrets in their stiff quadrille. Parents nod
and watch their children watch the bloodshed
always about to happen: the wee mouse
cower, the wildcat locked in a pointless
leap. It was Bosch, I think, who painted
the Cat padding into Eden with a small beast
limp in her mouth. A child smiles. Her father
aims a camera. He shoots, and does not ask
what the half-silvered hare asserts,
stopped on the cusp of change, forever
almost escaping, kicking his heels at the dark.

The Currs

(*in memoriam* Julianna Curr,
died 1834, Stanley, Tasmania)

Edward named the sands for home
– *Edgecombe, Hellyer, Montagu* –
the isthmus where the town would be,
Stanley for his patron. He called
the convicts *government men*
working for him *on assignment*.
He was *Master of the Company*.

The house was from a pattern book:
a rectory with veranda. He planted
pines to hide the glossy sea,
gorse, a hedge of English hawthorne,
built a clapboard chapel for the men,
basalt stables for the horses. The bride
was seventeen, from Dorset.

She saw the country paled through the swathes
of her wedding veil. *Terra nullus*:
vague, sun-dazzled land, flecked
with man-shaped shadows.
Gulls cry all night, Mama, she wrote.
They fear the cat, dear Edward says.
The moon is near, and yellow as a lamp . . .

She tried to sketch the place to show her:
drew the ragged eucalypts as elms,
the pines as rows of flagpoles.
She smeared on cobalt for the sea
reached for water to dilute it,
then mouthed a howl, and doubled up.
Pallid rain trailed across the paper.

She was shut up then for months.
Edward called his daughter Julianna.
At two, he set her in a tiny cart,
drawn by a gentled half-dingo.
The child called her monster *pet*,
in turn, the chained men called her
chuck, little lady of the manor.

Because the hedge had grown so tall,
they could not see, but heard
the day the dog joined in the fight, forgot
its bulldog manners. Men in irons
cannot run, nor ladies in corsets.
Edward ran but didn't know, that once,
which thing to shoot, meanwhile

the little cart turned over.
Edward chased the curs beyond the cliffs,
shot the dingo in the mouth and eyes
as it writhed in its broken harness.
The mother knelt and ripped her veil
to wrap the baby's body. When she looked up,
the world was different colours.

She saw a ring of convict's bloodied feet,
and her name on their fetters. She thought
what *flesh* meant, *bone, a natural life,
a sentence*; then, strangely, of the bird
she'd seen as a bride on the Tamar River.
It circled them: familiar, fist-headed,
black. Edward called it a swan.

To a Lawyer

May your cows come home,
not singly,
not warm-breathed in the evening,
quietly to their paddock
past a hand-smoothed, wooden gate;

nor in hundreds,
with docked horns and whistling cowherd,
stamped hips and heavy udders,
soft-eyed and organized,
to pasture in your meadow;

may they come
in truckfuls, in planeloads and ships' holds,
with flecked sides and red eyes,
black-flanked and glistening,
a prairie-full, a continent, a cavalcade of cows.

The Rich

This is a note to remind you

that when you envy their lived-in loafers,
the warm tan ankles on ox-blood soles,
when you reach to tip over the chairload
of plump hams in ski slacks, or tighten
the knot of their casual cashmeres –

rise above it, remember

that the men grin grins as if locked in chin-ups,
the women's brows are arched like flautists'.
Their lives are led in pursuit of purpose,
and their eyes are the eyes of a tightrope-walker
who can stride out only, cannot look down.

With Angels

(for Jonathon McCree)

It might start with a wing-tip, snuck
in your palm, hard beneath down, shy
as the nose of a well-mannered dog.
Don't push it. Don't shove yourself
under his ticklish wing, you don't
want to rest on that smooth
damask chest, feel his crucifix
twitch with each shocked boyish breath.

Wings are for flying. Imagine them:
flapping above you, freezing the sweat
on your hunched naked legs. They'd
tug him back with each thrust
like whiplash, like disgust, they'd
wrench up your hips to the crux of a *y*,
or suddenly out, a cork from a bottle.
And you can't fly, there's no getting round it.

If you clambered on top and squatted
with your thighs squashed like chicken,
or if you tried sideways, wings soft
on your flanks as a conference of moths,
you'd press the patterned feathers
out of weaving, of whack, you'd watch
the wings bent beneath you crack
on their arches, quills buckle like metal,

and pain crack his face like egg-glaze
on a fresco; and so wouldn't it end
with you going down as always,
him crossing his wings like a screen
on his chest? And as he shook and looked
to God, one hand vague on your nodding head,
would he weep, the way men do,
but pearls, or hard smalt angel tears?

The Acolyte

Though you swear you are not
Simeon Stylites –
wouldn't spend, as he did,
half your life on a pillar,
crane-still amid acres
of Antiochian desert,
surveying a perfect
circumference of sunset,
and nearer to God
by a clear sixty feet –

I have found myself lately
dreaming of pulleys,
of yard arms, of bundles
of rope, the number
of Tupperware beakers of cordial,
of wax-papered triangles
of potted-meat sandwich
that a suspended
lunch bucket
could practically take.

And I sleep, in your absence,
turning and turning,
like the hand of a watch,
or a woman prostrate
at the foot of a glaring
white pillar, pursuing,
through noon and siesta,
the rotating shadow
of a foreshortened, athletic,
odd form at the peak.

Guenever

Queen Guenever, for whom I make here a little
mention, that while she lived she was a true lover,
and therefore she had a good end.
                    – Le Morte D'Arthur, Book XI

For who would have Sir Galahad
who could have his battered troubled Dad?
Would swap that wholesome holy boy
who works out in the sun all day,
polishes his sword, his spurs, his pecs,
pores over texts and hands out tracts,
smiles kindly when I try to flirt –
for his saturnine slouch-hat Papa,
asleep with his head on his rusting armour,
scarred hand cradling a scar?

There are no flies on Galahad
though plenty buzz around his Dad.
Gal slow-mos through his martial arts:
his father fells three mosquitoes dead
with a single slap at his string vest.
And I have seen Sir Lancelot
snatch a moth from its lamp-bound orbit,
cage it in his palm adroitly,
blow it dusty, puzzled, free –
and all the while keep his eyes on me.

Young Galahad we leave to God –
but I tell you, sir, no woman, none,
who has known this father and his son
would not choose to sit by Lancelot,
ogle at him in his cups,
hear him blurt out blurry secrets,
sluice his desperation deeper;
believe that she alone could touch
the thing he holds beneath his shirt
– his cracked-wide-open hardnut heart.

Amore, Amore

(for Clare)

A man from the Altai Republic
is ideal, really. As he speaks
mostly the Altai tongue,
a sparsely-latined form of Hun,
and your Russian's distinctly slim,
you must talk in such Italian
as he can croon from opera.

And as his land is landlocked,
accessible, some summers only,
by steamer up the Yangtze,
by creaking cog-wheel railway
over hills as round as topiary,
by immemorial goat-track
with your trunk on your head,

you must roll up your hammock,
start that trek to the cliff top where,
between cloudbursts, you can gaze
at his mountain, watch his rare
Altai cheeses swing and drip
in their muslin, hear him whistle
the notes of *amore*, over and over,

and *amore*, *amore*, go echoing back.

The Personals

The one with herpes sounded best –
who didn't mention Solvency,
nor *s.o.h.*, nor Arts Degree,
didn't say he'd *l.t.m.*
a younger lady, petite, slim,
n.s., South-East, for Arts Pursuits –
but talked of this secret sore of his,
his soiling, suppurative lust.

To a Doctor

I expect you hear a lot of hearts –
know human pulses like a map,
the sort where blinking lights flash up
the shortest route from *you are here*;

your stethoscope must daily read
which parts are clogging, flaccid,
dead, so you must have known,
and should have said, when

I laid my head on your starched chest
that all the things I thought I heard –
glad thump of an unlikely catch,
an antique horseman at full stretch,

the lift of train tracks changing route
from tunnelled dark to open sky –
were in fact the brisk mechanic click
of a searchlight checking empty fields.

Or less – a valve, a tiny door
switched briefly open, swiftly shut.

Speculation

The papers promised an eclipse:
the moon's black disc distinctly,
slowly, pushed part-way across the sun,
as a counter for reckless stakes
is slid circumspectly on another.

They added I should only watch,
backwards, through a cardboard box,
even supplied a diagram, numbered
those already blind. It rained
all afternoon, of course. It was not

till four o'clock that I went out
and saw, in the empty, silvered street,
a shadow on the shadowed light,
a scarf of dark, like smoke
from barricades of tyres. I thought

of how it is with us – I stare,
you turn away and flush, as if
from heat or a blinding glare.
We generate that sort of weight.
A thickening of the atmosphere.

Raspberries

The way we can't remember heat, forget
the sweat and how we wore a weightless
shirt on chafing skin, the way we lose
the taste of raspberries, each winter; but

know at once, come sharp July, the vein
burning in the curtain, and from that light
– the block of sun on hot crushed sheets –
the blazing world we'll walk in,

was how it was, your touch. Not the rest,
not how we left, the drunkenness, just
your half-stifled, clumsy, frightened reach,
my uncurled hand, our fingers, meshed,

– like the first dazzled flinch from heat
or between the teeth, pips, a metal taste.

Heliograph

(after *Lecture on a Shadow*)

This, my love, if we believe John Donne,
is the best we'll get, love's brief high noon –
       it seems we've just walked out
       blinking, pallid, ill-equipped,
sans sun cream, phrase book, hat
into a marble mezzogiorno square
       after years in a damp cloister.
       We tread the burning ground like cats,
    crush short shadows underfoot –
    I've never been much good with heat.
    I shake, and turn to you, and stick

nuzzling for a scrap of shade. From here
you're statuesque, but bleared –

there's too much sun. Hold me close –
and straight, we're here to pose
       for a photograph, a portrait
       on self-timer. We'll look like tourists,
I expect: crumpled, modern, lost
holding up incongruous thumbs
       under faces shadowed deep as skulls –
       hopelessly small and un-baroque.
    It's hard to smile in direct light.
    Let's shut our eyes, count down the ticks
    and when we open at the click, squint

and see, beyond the square, a gap of shade –
an arch, an opening, a colonnade of days.

Spell

If, at your desk, you push aside your work,
take down a book, turn to this verse
and read that I kneel there, pressing
my ear where on your chest the muscles
arch as great books part, in seagull curves,
bridging the seasounds of your heart,

and that your hands run through my hair,
draw the wayward mass to strands
as flat as scarlet silk-thread bookmarks,
and stroke my cheeks as if smoothing
back the tissue leaves from chilly,
plated pages, and pull me near

to read my eyes alone, then you shall see,
silvered and monochrome, yourself,
sitting at your desk, taking down a book,
turning to this verse, and then, my love,
you shall not know which one of us is reading
now, which writing, and which written.

Conquest

Like mapping the ocean with ribbons,
like sticking a flag on the moon,
like finding a new range of mountains
and deciding to split them
into right-angled regions
named for Scottish market towns,

is how I claim you now.
Oddly, I am optimistic,
animals and farmers nod
as I pass by, unreeling wire.
Beyond the cliffs, like tips of coral reefs,
my ribbons float on summer waves.

And at night, on the moon,
I am acrobatic and buoyant,
radioing triumph to mission control,
performing slow-motion
elephant dances to my flag
and the grand, indifferent stars.

The Converted

I shall go out, and proselytize for Love,
trail through the streets with a handcart of tracts,
stop in positions of maximum nuisance –
in chainstore doorways, station forecourts –
stand in my mac, long robe, sou'wester,
my sandwich-board reading *Ever/After*,
and gesticulate like a silent movie
to the rained-on cars, the damp commuters.

I shall corner vulnerable individuals –
lone late-night walkers, Bogart-watchers,
aged bridesmaids, balding ushers, anyone
struggling with too much luggage, anyone
red-eyed, at home, at the wrong time of day –
and tap their shoulders, grasp their elbows,
hiss, *my story could be yours, come
to our lecture on Cracking the Code,* and press

into reluctant hands my book of miracles:
Shakespeare's sonnets, 1–40, Nancy Mitford,
Cavalcanti, the letters of Sir Stanley Spencer
to his wife in her asylum, the graffittoed heart
of Herculaneum, which, it has been scientifically
proven, reappeared line for line in Granton
sixth-form loo. I shall beg them to read
and swear that everything, each word, is true.

Content

Like walking in fog, in fog and mud,
do you remember, love? We kept,
for once, to the tourist path, boxed in mist,
conscious of just our feet and breath,
and at the peak, sat hand in hand, and let
the cliffs we'd climbed and cliffs to come
reveal themselves and be veiled again
quietly, with the prevailing wind.

The NewHome Cabaret

'Tis not, as once appeared the world,
A heap confused together hurled,
All negligently overthrown,
Gulfs, deserts, precipices, stone;
Your lesser world contains the same
But in more decent order tame;
You, Heaven's centre, Nature's lap
And Paradise's only map.

– From 'Upon Appleton House'
by Andrew Marvell

Upon No. 30

This house has seen no architect.
You aren't supposed to squint
at its magnificence, blink
at its postmodern wit, but,
as you walk home with lowered head,
glimpse it, brick and whole and low,
from the corner of the noisy road,
and nod, be comforted.

It was boshed up to fit
such space as could be bought for it
and stands with elbows doucely tucked
inches from the neighbours' path.
It was shaped, if shaped at all,
on the idea that a house should have
one front parlour and one back,
two window eyes, its own front door.

No wall is straight or angle right,
for it was measured out by feet
placed heel to toe in tightrope style,
while estimates of heights were made
with bricks and string and one shut eye;
someone lay flat to calculate
a bed-length in the upstairs room,
reached out to add a wardrobe's width.

Someone rather short, in fact.
We've grown since then –
this home for ten Victorians
will barely fit the two of us.
Let's go in, and hope a house
built from dirt with man's bare fists
has learned by now a woman's habit
of giving out, and being elastic,

so that the bowed wall will curve
a little more to let us breathe,
and the sloping floor will send
me on my office chair swivelling back
to meet your arms, and love rise
through each plaster pore, irreparable
as damp, and spread its spores
on every joist, invisibly, perpetually.

The NewHome Cabaret

Though we mean to plane
the walls to bone, pare the floorboards
bare and stain them dark, expose
expanses of Old Oxford bricks, raise
the grain in the tongue and groove,
to polish, bleach, limewash the lot
in the best spare modern style

we shall leave the 'fifties cooker
grinning where it stands.
It's labelled *NewHome Cabaret*,
the enamel sink is *Leisure*: we like
their cool design, bold notes of chrome
and the suggestion of undressing
in their aluminium names.

Underlay

Because we like to get things plain
we've hacked all day at nails and prised up
tacks and peeled and rolled and stacked
the soft strata of the floor. Now we sit on them,
a squashed pyramid of futures, and rest
our feet on the pale ghost-rug

the final oilcloth left. It was light to lift,
worn to the weft, but, where we scraped off
the dirt, still pink, still printed with chinoiserie:
a little lacquered bridge so clouded grey
with working boots that it no longer reached
the jasmine-cloaked pagoda.

It's dark, and in the window frame we see
ourselves, floating on a plane of light, haloed
in electricity, strange as if that first family
had looked up to see, briefly before them,
milk-skinned and alien, unimaginably large,
the future, fortunate, children of no war.

Hardboard

Grace Ethel Coombes covered up
the banisters and fireplaces,
the panels of the doors
in August, nineteen fifty-four
according to the crumpled *Mirror*

wedged in the bedroom chimney
behind the high-gloss paint
and hardboard, the tiny copper nails.
She was the aged daughter of this house.
Modern Housewives' War on Dust

the paper said, and *A Retraction*.
I tugged it out to see the picture,
and an avalanche of ash
fell in my lap and on the top
flopped the skeleton of a bird. Its skull

snapped off and lay wide-eyed.
A starling, or perhaps a thrush,
but shrunk to archaeopteryx.
Its wings were long white fingers,
stretched out to me in prayer.

Grace Ethel must have heard it fall
and thrash: a rush like love, at first,
then a nagging, migrainous pulse,
then a flutter like a faulty valve
in the chimney's hidden ventricle;

and pitied it, of course, but how
could she let that black
and headlong ball of soot fly out
to take its chance of air and light
or a swift bright death against her panes?

Dust

We've stripped this house to dust, my love,
the walls have pores like nibbled cake,
the ceilings crumb like icing;
the wood-wormed boards are light
as *langues de chat*, sugared with plaster.
And if you gather up the stuff,
and sift it from hand to hand,

you can see that of the larger grit,
bits must be brick and scraps of slate
from the gables and the chimney stack,
and since the wind blows east,
parts are shaved from St Mary's Church,
with one millionth, perhaps,
from the Holy Land or the Blue Mosque;

while of the finer, whiter stuff,
that silts our teeth and lines the bath,
some must be, already, us,
with a larger portion rubbed
from Miss Grace Coombes and all her folk
who lived here long enough to shed
themselves a hundred times at least.

Now we've sealed one room
with a skin of paint, knocked the worst
between the boards, laid a mattress
on the sloping floor. The heating ticks.
The ceiling shifts. Something leaks
behind the light, falls on our sheet, sparse
as the first sand in an upturned hourglass.

Customer Care

The man from Pickford's Movers
has wrapped my tin-opener
(bought from Price-Busters
and greased with years of tuna)
in six layers of tissue paper
and a corrugated tube.

On this same principle
were Tutankhamun's viscera,
liver, kidneys and brains,
bottled in four amphorae
and placed in alabaster
serpent-and-jackal-headed sculptures

of narrow, swaddled gods
which were huddled together
and left to gaze for all eternity
at each point of the compass
from the plump circumference
of a hieroglyphed pink pot.

Neither Pickford's nor Egyptians
consider it their place
to discriminate in packing
or in any way pass judgement
on what is vital to the new life
and what is obsolete.

The Mirror

The day we bought and gilded it,
it lay like a lake in my tiny flat,
showing us, as we rubbed its surface,
its stock of lover's secrets – vast,
grasping hands, dark nostril gaps,
our pendulous strange undersides,
front-lit, like a Lucien Freud.

Here, we've left it propped, let it
catch us out in bits – eyes bruised
with soot, hair aged with paint,
balletic legs on wobbling steps –
until now, the day to set it straight.
We're up against the glass, nose
to nose with our doubled selves.

I'm acting as the brace, spreadeagled
over the fireplace. You're on a chair,
mouth full of screws. We shake
with so much luck and glass, the risk
of arching past ourselves in showers
of shards and ancient mercury.
I shut my eyes, and feel the weight

go from me. You pull back my arm
and show me us. Fixed-up, framed,
hands raised and clasped – the Arnolfinis
at a football match. Behind us,
new-painted walls recede,
finished, levelled, green. The cat
curls his tail at the vanishing point.

The Tree

The apples are already ripe
on the tree Miss Coombes left us.
The tree is bowed almost to the ground.
I hadn't understood till now
the cold weight of them, or how
they crowd each branch in pairs,
yellow, round as Chinese lamps
on a ceremonial highway.

Dusk, and you're coming home.
I imagine your bike's dynamo
drawn like a fuse through
the darkening streets, to light
our house as now, all down our road,
the lights go on – the gold
of bulbs in potting sheds, ingots
of a hall, back bedroom, stair.

We live here now, and though,
elsewhere, a girl is leaning
on a carriage window, her finger
twisted round the rucksack packed
with everything she owns –
this is enough. We are
the lights, the lights, the lights
the trains flick by in the dark.

Present

For you, each night, the detail of each day:
so take the light that fell on London
this evening when I was on
the suburban, steady-breathing train.
Tender but particular, it rendered
brickwork and new leaves distinct,
gilded allotments and long gardens,
backlit tar-paper sheds,
filled failures of verandas,
with their intended, hopeful shape.

Caught the scarlet-chested builder
spading gravel in the mixer,
made him heroic, a war poster;
lent to blazered boys on platforms
blowing smoke rings bright as halos,
the child who trailed her sister
like a slow-to-take-off kite, to the one
hand-fasted couple, their flowered acne
and pram, to all their separate ritual
squabbles, an authentic air of idyll.

Later, take the contents
of each lit window that I passed,
that seemed, tonight, bright slides
of an ideal life, take the cool
of my arms without my coat,
on this, the first of no-coat days,
the warmth of the pub, and the glass
after glass of pure foam, pure gas,
the barman drew from the tap,
his laugh. And lastly take, my love,

the water main that burst and made
a fountain, this drab street Italian.
Adults, luckless since they are not us
stopped and tutted at the waste,
but the blast arched on regardless,
the top droplets golden in the lamp,
a flood of unstoppable coins. Take them.
I turned like Whittington, stood
with laughing children, still as Cortés
on his peak. I filled my pockets up.